THE GRADUATED SWING METHOD

THE GRADUATED SWING METHOD

RICHARD METZ

CHARLES SCRIBNER'S SONS · NEW YORK

Photos of Sam Snead, Gary Player, and Tom Weiskopf on pages 106–111 by Leonard Kamsler.

Library of Congress Cataloging in Publication Data

Metz, Richard, 1938–
    The graduated swing method.

    1. Swing (Golf)   I. Title.
GV979.S9M48   796.352'3   81-1538
ISBN 0-684-16868-5   AACR2

1 3 5 7 9 11 13 15 17 19   Q C   20 18 16 14 12 10 8 6 4 2

Printed in the United States of America

To Charles Scribner, Jr.

I want to thank Vince Harding
for all his valuable assistance with this book,
Peter Levy for his fine photography, and, finally,
Louise Ketz, my editor, who helped
me put it all together.

CONTENTS

THE GRADUATED SWING METHOD
What It Is and What It Does

The Graduated Swing Method, or GSM, is an innovative way to learn how to play golf or to improve your game. It is a straightforward presentation of golf fundamentals in a new, easily digested form. Departing from conventional teaching methods in which a full swing is learned first, the Graduated Swing Method begins with a miniature swing, or miniswing as I call it, that is gradually increased into a full swing. The GSM is a plan that takes you step by step through a series of lessons—from the time you learn how to grip the golf club until you make your first full swing at the ball. You will build up to a full backswing instead of beginning with it. By utilizing a miniswing at first as a base or foundation, you will find it much easier to start hitting the ball immediately. Then, by progressing step by step into a full swing, you will begin to feel at the outset how to make the proper movements with your body and how to swing the club with the hands and arms to produce good shots. Some of these fundamentals will be practiced without actually hitting a golf ball, but by the time the ball is added much of the mystery of the golf swing will have been dispelled and you will be able to progress with ease and confidence.

When I first started teaching, I soon found that few, if any, golf students were able to concentrate simultaneously on the several different movements of the body and swing the club freely at the same time. For that reason I became convinced that there must be a better teaching formula than the conventional one of undertaking the backswing, the downswing, and the follow-through all at the same time. For teaching purposes, I felt it would be far more logical to begin with a miniature swing, lengthen it step by step, practice each step, and only then incorporate them into a full swing, after each step had been perfected sufficiently. My strong conviction on this score brought about a departure from conventional methods, and I concentrated on developing the Graduated Swing Method.

The GSM, therefore, did not evolve by chance. It came about only after a great deal of experimentation and a search for the simplest and easiest way for my students to learn. It was adopted as standard procedure in my New York studio only after thousands of test cases had proved the method to be sound.

As a matter of fact, in a number of other sports that require precise form, such as skiing, skating, swimming, and diving, methods similar to the GSM have been used for many years. Isolating the critical important movements in these sports has also proved effective and enabled the sportsperson to practice the movements until they became second nature.

Further confirmation of the effectiveness of the Graduated Swing Method as a plan for learning came when I began studying the really good golf swings and noticed a marked similarity among all fine players. Their styles and physical sizes may have been different, but their swing fundamentals were very much alike. When one of these fundamentals soured, the good players immediately tackled the problem on the practice tee; their routines were usually identical.

First, the golfer would find the trouble; second, he would

isolate it from the rest of the swing. This isolation fascinated me. Why did these fine players do it? Because it made it easier for them to successfully repair the flaw before they put it back in the swing. The repetition of this routine by so many players convinced me that the golf swing could be learned or improved by everyone in much the same way.

Contrary to popular opinion, no one is born with a "natural" golf swing—not even Ben Hogan, Jack Nicklaus, or Sam Snead. The correct form must be learned. Of course, excellent coordination is an important advantage and may shorten the learning process, but anyone with average physical abilities can learn to play golf through the Graduated Swing Method, once he understands how to go about it and devotes a reasonable amount of time to practicing.

THE KEY SEGMENTS OF THE SWING

The GSM isolates five key segments of the golf swing: the miniswing (or hitting area), the half follow-through, the full follow-through, the half backswing, and the full backswing. These segments establish a logical progression that is easy to follow. You will be using a valuable checkpoint system by which you will know immediately whether or not you are in the correct position.

Lesson One deals with the proper way to grip the club. Lesson Two teaches you how to aim and position your body. In Lesson Three you will learn how to make the miniswing, which will serve as the foundation on which the full swing will be built. Once the miniswing becomes familiar, Lesson Four will show you how to gradually lengthen the miniswing forward into a full follow-through. This gradual building of the swing helps you to acquire the feel and awareness of the correct movements so that they can be repeated. When the full follow-through can be performed accurately with reasonable regularity, you will proceed to building a full backswing, in Lesson Five. Lesson Six focuses on how to combine the backswing, downswing, and follow-through into a fluid, full golf swing.

Because of the fundamental nature of the GSM approach, the following pages should prove useful to golfers on all levels—the beginner who has never held a club before, the high-handicap player who must alter his swing to improve his game permanently, and the good player searching for a simpler way to identify, locate, and remedy an error before it becomes a habit.

Golf would really be an easier game to learn if it were impossible to hit a good shot with a bad swing. If it were, one would always know whether or not one was swinging correctly. The Graduated Swing Method is designed to do just that, by making swing fundamentals so familiar that any departure from the standard will feel wrong and can be corrected. Being able to recognize the correct positions at key checkpoints and having the opportunity of returning to them at any time helps to identify an error and eliminate it.

Bear in mind that good golf is not a "do your own thing" game. Every golfer, according to his own size, has a correct or ideal swing pattern. Any deviation from the fundamentals of the golf swing compromises the chances for consistency. Also damaging is the tendency to employ fundamentals in a piecemeal fashion: "Hold your head steady"; Keep your left arm straight"; "Start the clubhead back low to the ground"; "Finish the swing"; and so on. Although each of these remedies has value, used alone or misused, they rarely help. As a consequence, when on the course, a player will fluctuate between very good days and very bad days. With any kind of swing one can occasionally hit a good shot. But with proper swing fundamentals, play and practice will help achieve a respectable, repeatable, consistent swing. This is what the Graduated Swing Method is designed to accomplish.

Every day in my New York studio I work with golfers of widely varying skills, and I have found that without exception my method of teaching can be applied to all. By using the GSM I have helped to build new golf swings, correct and rebuild faulty ones, and improve fundamentally good swings. I am confident that the Graduated Swing Method will work equally well for you, regardless of your own personal golfing status, and that it will speed you along to a better, more rewarding, and more enjoyable golf game.

BEFORE YOU BEGIN

Whenever any of us starts to learn a new skill, we want to progress as quickly as possible. This is understandable, but in learning the golf swing patience will bring many rewards. The beginning golfer generally wants to move along too quickly. He is prematurely concerned with hitting the ball, instead of concentrating on developing a proper swing. When hitting the ball is the most important thing to a player, his natural instincts will usually carry him in the wrong direction, away from the properly coordinated swing that is essential to making good golf shots. If you concentrate on correct form, in the long run you will make the most rapid progress.

For the golfer who has been playing for some time, the Graduated Swing Method can serve as an excellent review of your swing, as you move along in the six lessons. Left-handers can apply everything in the following pages simply by reversing the direction indicated and carrying on from the "port" side.

Beginners and experienced golfers alike will gain the most from this book by combining each lesson with as much actual practice as possible. Understanding each lesson as you read it is not enough, since the muscles of your body must be taught, too. Only after a good deal of practice will the muscles automatically execute the various movements of the golf swing. If this were not true, all we would have to do is study motion pictures of some of the golf greats—such as Littler, Weiskopf, Watson, or Miller—and then mimic their moves. Unfortunately, it just can't be done that way. As in the learning of other skills—whether they are simple ones like tying a knot or more complex, such as skiing—learning a sound golf swing takes practice. The only way to transform a movement that feels unnatural into one that is easy and familiar in the shortest possible time is by practice and more practice.

With the GSM, it is important that certain skills be acquired in each lesson and practiced before going further. When each fundamental feels easy and familiar, only then is it wise to move on to the next lesson.

The amount of equipment necessary to proceed with the GSM is minimal. You will need a golf club, preferably a short iron such as a number 9 or a pitching wedge. If you plan to work indoors, a small, inexpensive chip-and-drive mat with a built-in rubber tee is ideal. A plastic practice ball, or "whiffle" ball, will be fine for your first few lessons. Finally, a full-length mirror attached to a wall or door, or even simply propped up against a wall, door, or chair will prove extremely helpful in seeing for yourself exactly what you are doing and if you are doing it correctly.

Beyond the club, ball, and mirror (and the mat, if you're working indoors), nothing else is required except those personal attributes that I hope you have on hand in abundance—an inquisitive, open mind, a desire to learn, and a willingness to work (that is, practice). With these, I am confident that there will be no limit to what the Graduated Swing Method can help you accomplish in golf.

THE GOLF GRIP

None of the fundamentals of the golf swing is unimportant, but one of the most vital is how to grip a club correctly. It may seem unusual to beginners that so much emphasis is placed on how to hold a golf club properly. Certainly most people have no problem in gripping a tool, such as a hammer, the right way; one does it with little or no thought. But the golf grip is unique in that no other implement, whether for sports or for work, is held in quite the same way.

Why is the golf grip so important? Why does it deserve such meticulous attention? The answer is that the grip controls the angle of the clubface through the swing and allows the club to return to a square position without conscious effort. Even though both the shape and direction of a swing itself may be sound, if the clubface angle is wrong because of an incorrect grip, the ball simply cannot be hit consistently in the direction it is aimed.

Beginners may be confused by the terms "angle of the clubface" and "square position," but these two essentials will be explained in detail in the next section.

Just like the other fundamentals of the swing, the golf grip evolved through years of trial and error. The most pop-

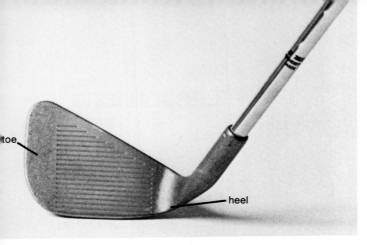

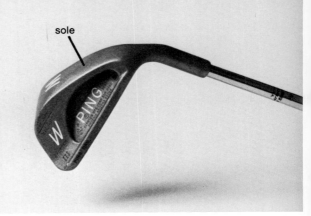

A view of the clubface showing the heel and the toe.   A view of the back of a golf club showing the sole.

ular grip, the overlapping, has received such universal acceptance (although it is far from being an "obvious" way to hold the club) that it still bears the name of the famous English golf champion, Harry Vardon, who first made it popular. A correct grip was important to him and his peers in his day (beginning in the 1890s), and it is of equal importance to you today.

THE TARGET LINE
AND A SQUARE CLUBFACE

Before we start on the proper grip, it is necessary first to introduce two important terms and what they mean. The first is the "target line" of a golf shot, the second, the "square clubface."

The target line, or the intended line of flight, is an imaginary line that runs from the ball to the spot where you want it to land. It is easiest to find the target line by standing a few yards behind the ball facing your target. Line up your ball with your target, much as a rifleman aligns the sights on his gun. When the club is set down properly behind the ball with the proper grip, with the leading edge of the clubface forming a perfect right angle to the target line, this position is called a square clubface.

Far too few golfers—other than expert players—make it a habit on every shot of finding their target line and making

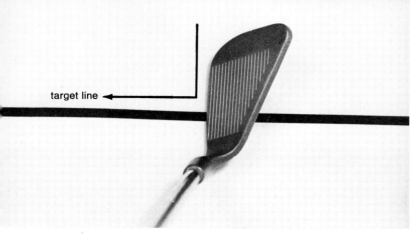

target line

When the clubface is square to the target line, the leading edge of the clubface forms a perfect right angle to the target line.

sure that the clubface is square to the line. Taking the time for this routine will pay high dividends as you move along with your lessons and when you actually begin to play.

The two most common errors in placement of the club-head are called an "open clubface" and a "closed clubface." In the correct, or "square" clubface, the bottom leading edge of the clubface is perpendicular (that is, square) to the target line. When the clubface is "open," the heel of the clubhead is ahead of the toe upon impact with the ball. An open clubface will cause the ball to go to the right of your target. When the clubface is "closed," the toe of the clubhead is ahead of the heel at impact. A closed clubface will cause the ball to go to the left of your target.

When the clubface is "open," the heel of the club-head is ahead of the toe upon impact. This incorrect placement will cause the ball to go to the right of your target.

When the clubface is "closed," the toe of the club-head is ahead of the heel upon impact. This incorrect placement will cause the ball to go to the left of your target.

GRIP OF THE LEFT HAND

To grip the club correctly, it is necessary to start with a square clubface. The bottom of the clubhead (the sole) should lie flat on the ground with neither the toe nor the heel tilted upward.

Begin by placing your left hand on the grip of the club close to the butt end so that the shaft lies diagonally across your palm. The lower part of the club, where it crosses your palm, should touch the first joint of your index finger. The upper part of the club should come to rest just under the muscle pad at the inner heel of your left hand.

Now close the fingers of your left hand around the club. If you do this properly, you will be holding the club in the palm and fingers, not the palm alone or the fingers alone. The thumb should be resting on top of the grip. If it is, and your placement of the club is right (a square clubface), the back of your left hand should now be parallel to the leading edge of the clubface. Make every effort to coordinate the two things—correct grip and square clubface—because they belong together; one is not right without the other.

Although the club is held firmly with all the fingers, you should grip more securely with the last three fingers of your left hand. This will press the shaft against the palm just below the muscle pad. The left thumb, which you positioned on top of the shaft, should be extended, allowing no space between the club and the thumb.

Looking down at your left hand, you will notice a line that is formed by your upper left thumb and index finger. If extended, this line should point to your right eye. Also, as you look down you should see the knuckle at the base of your index finger, if your left hand is positioned correctly. If more than one knuckle is visible or if the line formed by your

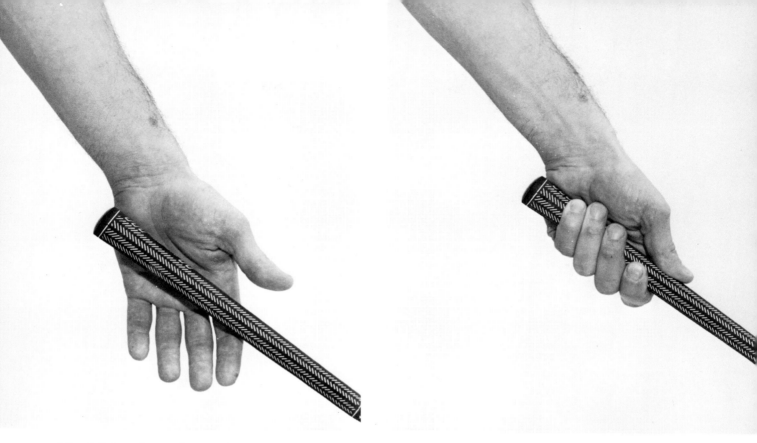

The left-hand grip begins by placing your hand close to the butt end of the club. The lower part of the club, where it crosses your palm, should touch the first joint of your index finger.

If you close the fingers of your left hand around the club properly, you will be holding the club in the palm *and* fingers, not the palm alone or the fingers alone. The thumb should be resting on top of the grip.

thumb and index finger points to the right of your right eye, it indicates that your left hand is too far to the right on the club. This "strong" position may cause a closed clubface when you swing, and the ball will fly to the left of its target. A "weak" position is just the opposite, occurring when the left hand is placed too far to the left on the club. In a weak position you will be unable to see the first knuckle of your left hand, and the thumb-and-index-finger line will point to the left of your right eye, which will cause an open clubface when you swing, so that the ball will be hit to the right of your target.

Even though most of us associate the terms "strong" and "weak" with "good" and "bad," when applied to the golf grip that interpretation is not necessarily true. "Strong" simply

 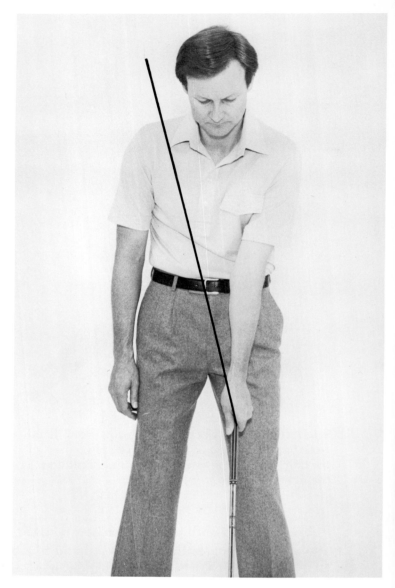

With a proper left-hand grip, you will notice a line formed by your upper left thumb and index finger. If this line is extended, it should point to your right eye.

One type of improper left-hand grip is known as a "strong" position. If more than one knuckle is visible or if the line that is formed by your thumb and index finger points to the right of your right eye, your left hand is too far to the right on the club.

Another type of improper left-hand grip is the "weak" position, in which the left hand is placed too far to the left on the club. In a weak position you will not be able to see the first knuckle of your left hand, and the line formed by your thumb and index finger will point to the left of your right eye.

means that the hands are placed to the right on the club; "weak" indicates that the hand position is more to the left. Either extreme is undesirable and should be avoided.

The proper left-hand grip is particularly important because the position of your left hand on the club will help you establish the correct right-hand grip.

Before going on to the proper grip for the right hand, it will be to your advantage to practice placing the left hand on the club and repeating the process until it becomes familiar and begins to feel comfortable.

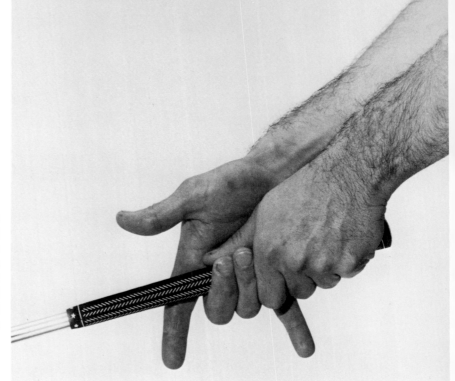

To begin the right-hand grip, place the first joints (tnose closest to your palm) of the ring, middle, and index fingers on the club with the ring finger as close as possible to the index finger of the left hand. The palm of your right hand should now be facing the left palm and be parallel to the leading edge of the clubface.

GRIP OF THE RIGHT HAND

The left-hand grip is a palm-and-finger grip; the right-hand grip is almost entirely a finger grip. To begin, place the first joints (those closest to your palm) of the ring, middle, and index fingers on the club with the ring finger as close as possible to the index finger of the left hand, which is already in place. The palm of your right hand should now be facing the left palm and be parallel to the leading edge of the clubface.

Close these three fingers around the club, with the ring finger and middle finger of the right hand gripping the club more firmly than does the index finger.

As for the placement of the little finger of the right hand, there are two possibilities. The most popular one, which is also my preference, is called the "overlapping" grip. It locks the right little finger securely in the groove between the left index finger and middle finger knuckles. This overlapping position allows the hands to function more as one. An alternative is the "interlocking" grip. This variation enables the golfer with short fingers to position his hands close together by placing the little finger of the right hand between the left index finger and middle finger. The little finger then wraps around the base of the index finger. Other than this minor change, the position of the hands on the club is the same as that in the overlapping grip.

Once the four fingers of the right hand are in place, all that remains is for you to fold your right hand on top of your left thumb. The left thumb will fit snugly into the palm of your folded right hand, which conceals the thumb entirely.

It is important that the fleshy part of your right thumb above the large knuckle press down on the left thumb. This will help to keep your hands together and prevent any loos-

There are two possibilities for placement of the little finger of the right hand. In the overlapping grip, the right little finger is locked securely in the groove between the left index finger and middle finger knuckles.

In the interlocking grip, the right little finger is placed between the left index and middle fingers. The little finger then wraps around the base of the index finger.

ening of your right hand from the club during the swing. The right thumb pad should rest on the left side of the shaft, with the thumb and index finger touching or very nearly so. If your right thumb sticks out beyond the right index finger, it is an indication that you are holding the club in the palm of your right hand and not in the fingers.

Notice the line that is formed by your right thumb and the upper part of your right index finger. This line should point to your right eye.

GRIP WITH BOTH HANDS

Now that you have the hands on the club, it is important to remember that the hands must fit closely together so that they can work as a unit. The farther apart the hands are, the more they will move independently. The proper grip helps to eliminate any opposing action between the two hands.

Be sure that you are not holding the club too tightly. A firm but flexible grip is necessary in placing the hands correctly and is essential for an effective swing. Flexibility in the grip also makes it much easier to maintain the correct hand position throughout the swing. Since individuals differ considerably in the strength of their hands, it is difficult to say with certainty exactly what is too tight. But in all cases, the pressure applied should be much like a friendly handshake—not too limp, but not a bone crusher either. Flexibility in the fingers is essential for golfers no matter what their hand strength. Wearing a golf glove on the left hand is a good idea, since it helps maintain a more secure grip without having to hold the club too tightly. (For clarity, the pictures in this book show the left hand without a glove.)

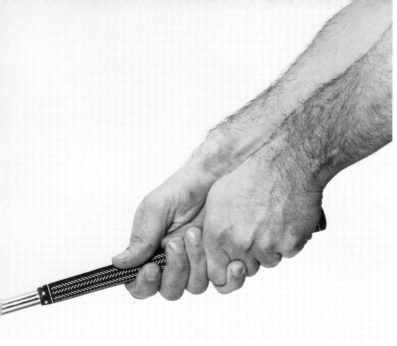

It is important in the correct grip that the fleshy part of your right thumb press down on the left thumb. The right thumb pad should rest on the left side of the shaft, with the thumb and index finger touching or very nearly so.

Remember that in the correct grip your two hands must fit closely together so that they can work as a unit. Be sure that you are not holding the club too tightly. A firm but flexible grip is necessary in placing the hands correctly and is essential for an effective swing.

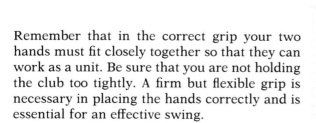

A common misconception is that there is less chance of grip slippage during the swing if the club is held very tight. More often than not, the opposite is true. Fingers that are too tight or inflexible on the club may prevent the hands and wrists from acting as they should during the swing. In most cases, loosening of the hands on the club becomes a substitute for proper wrist action, described in later lessons. Any loosening of this kind may cause a regripping of the club at some point in the swing, making it almost impossible to maintain a square clubface.

It is almost certain that you will find the correct golf grip unnatural and even uncomfortable at first. But if you practice the grip for a few minutes a day, it will begin to feel more familiar and soon your grip will become second nature. At this point you can be assured that you have learned this important fundamental thoroughly.

When you practice gripping, your first step should be the ever-important square clubface. Then see what the hands look like together, and get the feel of your hands close to each other and the feel of the clubhead. The more often you repeat the correct grip, the more natural it will become. Remember, too, that flexibility in the hands is essential for a good golf grip.

AIMING AND SETTING UP TO THE BALL

Once you have become familiar with the correct golf grip, the next step is to learn how to "set up to the ball"—that is, how to position the club and your body in relation to the ball. Remember that the imaginary line that extends through the ball to the target is the target line, or intended line of flight, and that when the clubface is square to the target line, perpendicular to it, it is aimed at the target.

Golf is essentially a target game. The ball is hit from the teeing ground to the fairway and from the fairway onto the putting green. The fairway and the putting green are the targets. (Unfortunately, in between there are often monstrous hazards such as bunkers, trees, lakes, and streams intended to thwart you.) The point, of course, is that it is hardly worthwhile to hit a golf ball far or even straight if it isn't going to come to rest reasonably close to the intended target.

Aiming and setting up to the ball should become a routine. Good players are extremely deliberate in aiming the clubface and taking their stance. Jack Nicklaus and Gary Player immediately come to mind as golfers who take great care with these essential preliminaries. The next time you watch the touring pros, either in person or on television, watch for and note their meticulous routine. Aiming and setting up properly are among the easiest of the fundamentals the beginner has to learn, because this is simply a matter of remembering what is necessary and then taking the time to do it carefully.

To find the target line, stand about ten feet behind the ball, facing your target. If you stand too close to the ball, you will not get a good perspective on the ball's intended flight. To help you visualize the line of flight more accurately, place a golf club on the ground in front of the ball to represent the target line. Once you have determined the target line, you are almost ready to set up to the ball.

POSTURE

Before you can actually set up to the ball, you must establish the proper posture, which can best be learned by using a step-by-step routine.

First, stand erect with your feet spread apart shoulder width and with your arms hanging naturally at your sides. Pull the shoulders back, the stomach in, and keep your eyes straight ahead. Next, bend forward from the waist, being careful to keep your back straight. To assume this bent position and maintain your balance, your backside has to stick out a little. The result is a kind of formal bow, much like that which the Japanese perform so gracefully. This position is extremely important, because it allows your shoulders to tilt properly as they turn in the swing.

Hold your head high enough so that your shoulders will have room to turn when you start to swing. (Golfers who wear bifocals must hold the head as high as good vision permits.) Next, making sure your backside still sticks out, slightly flex

To assume the proper posture for the golf swing, begin by standing erect with your feet spread apart shoulder width and your arms hanging naturally at your sides. Pull the shoulders back, the stomach in, and keep your eyes straight ahead.

Next, bend forward from the waist, being careful to keep your back straight. To assume this bent position and maintain your balance; your backside has to stick out a little. This position is extremely important, because it allows your shoulders to tilt properly as they turn in the swing.

Making sure that your backside still sticks out, slightly flex your knees, which will tend to remove any tension in the legs and allow them to move more easily. Now, assume a slightly knock-kneed position to ensure that the weight is evenly distributed toward the inside of the feet.

your knees, which will tend to remove any tension in the legs and will allow them to move more easily. Now, assume a slightly knock-kneed position to ensure that the weight is evenly distributed toward the inside of the feet.

When you have bent forward from the waist and your knees are in the proper position, you will find that your weight is between the balls of your feet and your heels, as well as toward the inside of your feet. Your weight should be evenly distributed between both feet. You should feel that your legs are alive and ready to spring into action. Note from the illustrations that the proper setup position is a series of straight lines and angles, with no curves.

Practice establishing the correct posture using this step-by-step routine until it feels comfortable. Then you are ready to set up to the ball.

THE SETUP POSITION

Standing behind the ball on the target line, grip the club, making sure that both hands are properly placed. Approach the ball from the left side of the target line. Step forward with your right foot as you set the club down with its sole flat on the ground, with neither the toe nor the heel of the clubhead tilted up but with the leading edge directly behind the ball, square to the target line.

Now you are ready to adjust your left foot and your body so that your overall stance is correct in relation to the ball.

Assume the proper posture as you put your left foot into position. An imaginary line across your toes should be parallel to the target line.

Imagine for a moment a second line, perpendicular to the target line and just touching the back of the ball. Your feet

Always approach the ball from the left side of the target line.

Grip the club, making sure that both hands are properly placed, and step forward with your right foot.

Set the club down with its sole flat on the ground, with neither the toe nor the heel of the club-head tilted up but with the leading edge directly behind the ball, square to the target line.

should be set so that this second line is equidistant between your heels. The distance between your heels should be approximately the width of your shoulders.

The left foot should be toed out slightly to the left. This will make it easier to shift your weight over onto the left leg during the downswing. Your right foot should point straight ahead, or it may be very slightly toed out to the right. Be care-

Adjust your left foot and your body so that your overall stance is correct in relation to the ball. When you assume the proper posture, an imaginary line across your toes should be parallel to the target line. Another imaginary line, perpendicular to the target line and just touching the back of the ball, should be equidistant between your heels. An imaginary line across your shoulders, just like the line across your toes, must be parallel to the target line.

ful that the right foot does not toe out too much, since there is a danger of over turning your hips when you make your backswing, which will prevent you from winding your upper torso tight enough. (Full comment on this will follow in Lesson Five.)

The imaginary line across your shoulders, just like the line across your toes, must be parallel to the target line. Actually, this shoulder line is more vital in establishing the proper body position than is the placement of your feet, because the direction in which the club is swung will almost always follow the direction in which your shoulders are aligned. In the correct "square" stance, the imaginary lines across your toes, knees, hips, and shoulders are all parallel to the target line.

Most good golfers work themselves into their setup position following the preceding procedure. A common fault of high-handicap players is to reverse the procedure. That is, they set themselves up to the ball with their feet first and then set the club behind the ball. The best way to set up is to aim the clubface first and then position your feet and the rest of your body accordingly.

Next in the setup procedure is the position of your hands and arms. If you have bent forward from the waist a sufficient amount, you will be looking down and back in order to see your hands on the club. Imagine a vertical line from your eyes to the ground. As you look down, if any part of your hands is positioned on or beyond this line, your arms are too far from your body. In the proper position, the upper arms are close to the chest and should hang from the shoulders naturally. The chin is well off your chest. Your head should be positioned behind the ball—that is, the head is slightly to the right of the ball as you look down at it.

As they grip the club, your hands should be only far enough away from your body to have room to pass the upper legs comfortably. Here, again, there will be variations according to the golfer's height, length of the arms, and the length of the club.

In the correct setup position, the hands are also slightly ahead of the ball, enough so that your left arm and the shaft of the club form a straight line. This line is evident when viewed by someone in front of you and is what you would see yourself if you looked up into a mirror. From this angle the club becomes an extension of the left arm. You will notice, too, that since your right hand is below your left, your right shoulder is lower than your left.

The right arm is not straight but is slightly flexed at the elbow. Viewed from your right side as you address the ball, the right arm should be inside the left, that is, a little closer to your body. The entire upper right side of the body should be free from tension. This will make execution of the correct backswing and downswing easier.

Two logical questions can be asked at this stage: "Do I keep my feet the same distance apart for all shots?" and "Is the ball always in the same spot relative to my feet for all shots?" I have delayed comment on these basics until now because I felt that the standard aiming and setup procedures should come first.

In answer to the question on how far to keep your feet apart, the following is a good guide. Assuming that you are hitting with a number 5 iron, the distance between your heels should be approximately shoulder width. As the clubs get longer, moving up toward the driver, the space between the feet increases slightly; as the clubs get shorter, moving down toward the wedge, there should be slight decreases in the space between the feet. There are variations, of course, just as there are variations in player physique, width of shoulders, overall height, the length of the legs, and so on. The important point is that the stance should be wide enough to give you a solid base, but not one so wide that it becomes difficult to turn the body and shift your weight in a full swing.

As to the placement of the ball relative to the feet, the following guidelines should be of value. For the pitching wedge up through the number 5 iron, put the back of the ball on an imaginary line perpendicular to the target line and extending out from a point midway between your heels. From the number 4 iron up to the driver, the ball placement should

Use the following guidelines for ball placement relative to the feet. For the pitching wedge up through the number 5 iron, put the back of the ball on an imaginary line perpendicular to the target line and extending out from a point midway between your heels.

From the number 4 iron up to the driver, the ball placement should be on a similar line extending about 2 inches inside your left heel.

be on a similar line extending about 2 inches inside your left heel. Again, slight variations will occur as players differ and as they progress in their abilities. But for most golfers, these guideline positions will prove sound and serve very well.

Gripping the club, aiming, and setting up to the ball are very important. Because they are not as exciting as striking the ball or working on the subtleties of the swing, they are often skipped over in the early stages—but they are critically important and will justify your spending all the time necessary to master them properly.

A square stance is the basic body position for all full shots you will be making. Practice the stance in front of a mirror to be sure you are doing it properly.

Over the years I have seen many golfers who repeatedly gripped the club in a haphazard manner and did not bother to aim it or set up to the ball in the proper way. Some have been able to get away with an acceptable shot despite this carelessness, but not often. A lack of attention to these fundamentals puts two strikes on such players at the outset. If you take the time to learn how to grip, aim, and set up to the ball before you start thinking about hitting it, you will have laid a solid groundwork for an excellent swing.

THE MINISWING

The purpose of the golf swing is to deliver the clubhead squarely to the ball in the direction of the target and with maximum speed at the moment of impact. Sounds complicated, doesn't it? Well, it is, and to do it requires a sequence of perfectly coordinated movements.

When I first saw how difficult it is for a beginner to make the proper movements for a full swing all at once, I conceived the Graduated Swing Method. In this lesson of the GSM you will learn a miniature swing, or miniswing, that will gradually be extended (in later lessons) into a full swing. Success with the GSM has shown that the student must master the miniswing before he can be taught the full swing. This is much the same as mastering the scales on a piano or learning how to finger the various chords before attempting to play an entire musical piece. In this way, the GSM allows you to perfect each step in the building process, since the miniswing serves as a foundation on which to build your full golf swing.

Before starting on the miniswing, however, it is useful to take a brief look at the full swing. After all, that is the final goal of your instruction, and having a preliminary picture of the full swing in your mind will help during the building process.

The full golf swing, simply described, consists of a backswing and a downswing. In the backswing, the golfer swings the club back and up from the ball, coiling his upper body tightly, with the left shoulder under or slightly past the chin. In the downswing, the body uncoils and the club is swung down to hit the ball toward the target. The momentum of the club after it strikes the ball will carry the golfer into a natural follow-through.

You might look over some of the photographs of several great players beginning on page 101. Even though the pictures cannot show you continuous movement, they make it clear that the full swing requires carefully timed movements of the entire body.

But for now, we are concerned only with the hitting area of the swing—the miniswing area. If you carefully study the photographs on pages 101–113, you will notice that there are differences among some of the fine golfers at the top of their backswings and in their finishes. But if you look closely at the hitting areas, you will notice some marked similarities; they are almost all in identical positions.

Starting only with the hitting area of the swing, the miniswing, is the easiest way to begin your progress toward a full swing. The shortness of this little swing allows you to feel the muscle actions that are used to hit the ball off the ground with reasonable accuracy. The shortness of the miniswing also helps you to coordinate the lower body (feet, legs, hips) with the upper body (shoulders, arms, hands) while making the forward swing. This coordination is essential if you are to learn how to avoid golf's most common fault—swinging the club in the wrong direction, toward the left of the target. (Further comment on this fault is included in the discussion of the downswing.)

The miniswing can be broken down into two parts: the mini backswing and the mini forward swing.

THE MINI BACKSWING

The mini backswing is the initial takeaway movement of a full backswing. For now, we are concerned only with this part of the swing. Begin by gripping the club and setting up to an imaginary ball, just as you did in Lesson Two. Be sure that your grip is correct and that the clubface is square to the target line.

Start the mini backswing by pushing the clubhead straight back from the ball with an extended left arm. Keep the clubhead low to the ground, and do not allow it to come back more than 12 inches. As the clubhead moves back, the

Start the mini backswing by pushing the clubhead straight back from the ball with an extended left arm. Keep the clubhead low to the ground and do not allow it to come back more than 12 inches.

shoulders will start to turn, bringing the clubhead slightly inside the target line. There is no weight shift or movement of the lower body. There also is no wrist action in the mini backswing, so be sure that the back of your left hand, your left arm, and the shaft of the club maintain their straight-line relationship.

To repeat—you should start the mini backswing by *pushing* the clubhead straight back from the ball with an extended left arm. Make this movement slowly and deliberately. Throughout the mini backswing, your arms and hands should maintain their original position relative to your chest.

Practice the mini backswing and check yourself in a mirror. Watch for the following:

1. Are the hands, arms, and shoulders starting to move together? If they are, you are establishing a path along which the club moves. Consistency in the takeaway is partly responsible for making a good swing repeatable, or "grooved."

2. Is the clubhead starting to move straight back from the ball low along the ground? Try to avoid the common mistake of lifting the club abruptly with the right hand and arm.

3. Is the club moving away from the ball only the proper short distance—12 inches? Your mirror will help you answer this.

4. Has the lower body remained stationary? Here, again, your mirror will provide the answer. Your goal at this point is to have no movement of the lower body and no weight shift.

As you practice your mini backswing, remember that each fundamental in the GSM building process must be learned before going on to the next. Avoid the temptation to move ahead too quickly. Instead of helping you, moving on too soon may slow down your progress considerably.

THE MINI FORWARD SWING

"What's the most important move of the golf swing?" is probably the one question most frequently asked by students. Of course, there are no unimportant moves, but my best answer to the question would be the movement of the lower body, particularly that of the feet and legs, that starts the downswing.

In the GSM, it is essential to learn this fundamental lower body movement and how to coordinate it with the movements of the hands and arms as they swing the club. It must be mastered thoroughly before you can go on to a longer swing.

Although some tour professionals have unorthodox backswings, all successful players make the same lower body movement at the start of the downswing. It is that movement that we are concerned with now.

Basically, this movement involves pushing against the ground with the feet and a smooth, thrusting, lateral motion of both legs while, simultaneously, the arms and hands pull the club forward to hit the ball. The impression should be that the lower body is sliding out from under the torso. To perform this movement correctly, it helps to visualize the leg movement as primarily an action of the knees, for if the feet push against the ground and the knees slide to the left together, the rest of the lower body will follow naturally.

Later in this lesson is a discussion of how the mini forward swing fits into the full swing pattern, but for now just concentrate on how this movement of the legs is actually achieved.

A Helpful Exercise

Here is a useful exercise that will help give you the correct feeling of pushing properly with the balls of your feet and moving your legs and lower body at the start of the mini forward swing. Set up to an imaginary ball just as you did in Lesson Two, but instead of gripping the club, place the palms of both hands flat against the sides of your upper legs above the knees. From this stationary position, push the feet against the ground and slide both knees sideways to the left. Both arms are obviously forced to move with the legs. Some of your weight begins to shift to the outside of the left foot and back toward the heel, and the right shoulder will begin to tilt downward slightly. Check yourself in the mirror; be sure that as the lower body shifts to the left your head remains steady.

Up to this point, I have deliberately made no mention of the hips. Try the exercise, look again in the mirror, and notice that as the knees shift to the left the hips move too. Human anatomy guarantees that. The point is that if the legs move laterally in one (i.e., the correct) direction, it is unlikely that the hips will strike out on their own in the other (i.e., the wrong) direction.

This exercise is valuable as preparation for the mini forward swing, because it enables you to feel how the body should move with the arms in the proper direction.

Now let's add a golf club to the exercise. Grip the club properly and assume the correct setup position to an imaginary ball. With no backswing at all, push your feet against the ground and slide your knees sideways to the left as your arms and hands pull the clubhead along the target line. The clubhead should stay close to the ground and not pass forward of the imaginary ball more than 12 inches, the same length as that of the mini backswing. By holding the finish

A useful exercise to help you get the correct feel of pushing properly with the balls of your feet and moving your legs and lower body at the start of the mini forward swing begins by setting up to an imaginary ball. Place the palms of both hands flat against the sides of your upper legs above the knees.

From this position, push the balls of your feet against the ground and slide both knees sideways to the left. Both arms are obviously forced to move with the legs. Some of your weight begins to shift to the outside of the left foot and back toward the heel, and the right shoulder will begin to tilt downward slightly.

To begin the mini forward swing, grip the club properly and assume the correct setup position to an imaginary ball.

With no backswing at all, push with the balls of your feet against the ground and slide your knees sideways to the left as your arms and hands pull the clubhead along the target line.

and checking yourself in the mirror you will know immediately if your position is correct. At this point in your follow-through you will see that your chest has remained parallel to the target line and that the left arm and shaft of the club still form a straight line.

One of the best ways to make sure that you are making

The clubhead should stay close to the ground and should not pass forward of the imaginary ball more than 12 inches. At this point in your follow-through you will see that your chest has remained parallel to the target line and that the left arm and shaft of the club still form a straight line.

this move correctly is to watch your knees. Remember that when you first set yourself up for this exercise the imaginary line extending across the knees was parallel to the target line. If you move your legs and the rest of your lower body to the left correctly, the imaginary line across your knees will remain parallel to that line.

Another test to see if you are moving your knees correctly in the mini forward swing is to hold a club lightly across your knees.

Make the lateral knee move and check the club. If it's parallel to the target line, you are in the right position.

Here's another test to see if you are making this move correctly. Hold a club lightly across your knees. Make the lateral knee move again, and check the club. If it's parallel to the target line, you are in the right position. Conversely, if the knees have turned around to the left, instead of moving sideways, your right knee will have moved immediately outside

If after you make the lateral knee move your knees have turned around to the left, instead of moving sideways, your right knee will have moved immediately outside the left. This will also cause the right side of your body, particularly the right shoulder and arm, to turn counterclockwise and the club will be swung in the wrong direction—to the left of the target.

the left. This in turn will have caused the right side of your body (particularly the right shoulder and arm) to turn counterclockwise to the left instead of tilting down with both shoulders remaining parallel to the target line. The result of this improper move is that the club will be swung in the wrong direction—to the left of the target.

The importance of this lower body movement cannot be overemphasized. Moving the legs properly at the start of the downswing keys a coordinated movement of the upper body with the lower, thus making it easier for the arms and hands to swing the club in the right direction. The lower body must lead the upper on the forward swing.

Practice these exercises a few times and you will be ready to fuse a mini backswing and mini forward swing into one miniswing.

Try it.

COMBINING THE MINI BACKSWING AND MINI FORWARD SWING

Grip the club, preferably a 9 iron or pitching wedge, and set yourself up to an imaginary ball. Use a tee pushed well into the ground or a coin to represent the imaginary ball. Start the mini backswing with the arms and hands pushing the clubhead straight back no more than 12 inches. Remember, the clubhead will begin to move along the target line, but as your shoulders begin to turn, it will start to move inside. If your takeaway is correct, the relation between the back of your left hand, your left arm, and the shaft of the club will remain unchanged; it continues to form a straight line. The shaft is still an extension of the left arm.

Remember that so far there is no wrist action, no movement of the lower body or weight shift. Now start the forward swing by pushing the feet against the ground and sliding both knees sideways to the left, keeping the imaginary line across them parallel to the target line. Coordinate this action of the lower body with your arms and hands, pulling the clubhead back to and along the target line. The clubhead should not get ahead of the hands until after the imaginary ball is hit. Continue the swing in the same direction for a distance of 12 inches after the ball has been struck.

Repeat this miniswing with the imaginary ball several times, and check it in your mirror. If you are satisfied that you are doing it properly, you are ready to hit balls with the miniswing.

HITTING THE BALL WITH A MINISWING

At first, don't worry about how well you hit the ball. Concentrate on the shape of the swing and what it feels like to make the miniswing correctly. I advise hitting the balls off a tee (either rubber or wooden, depending on where you are practicing). A tee makes it much easier to hit the ball at first, and you will be free to concentrate on how to do it correctly.

Don't expect this miniswing to carry the ball very far or very high in the air—it can't and it shouldn't. What you are striving for is the feel of the swing and its proper shape.

There are several ways to determine whether or not you have made the miniswing correctly. Ask yourself these questions after you have tried the miniswing.

1. Did the ball go where it was aimed? If not, one of two errors probably occurred. You may have swung the club in the wrong direction, or the clubface may not have been square at the moment of impact. If the ball flew to the left, it will be helpful for you to feel that you are keeping the clubhead more inside the target line until making contact with the ball. Don't be afraid to exaggerate. Now check your position again. If the club is swung in the proper direction and the ball still goes to the left, you probably closed the clubface (toe ahead of heel at impact). Check your grip, clubface alignment, and proper square setup position before hitting each ball. Failure in any of these fundamentals can prevent you from hitting the ball straight.

2. Did the clubhead stay low to the ground on both backswing and forward swing? Keep the clubhead low as it moves along the target line on the backswing and on the "follow-through" after striking the ball—low enough to "sweep the dew off the grass." If you attempt to help the ball into the air by lifting the clubhead abruptly either on the backswing or forward swing or by allowing the clubhead to get ahead of your hands before impact with the ball, you will probably "top" it along the ground—the opposite of what you tried to do.

3. Is the finish correct at the end of this miniswing? If it is, your body is still parallel to the target line, your left arm and the shaft of the club still form a straight line, and the clubhead has moved only 12 inches or less along the target line beyond the ball's original position. As a result of your lower body initiating the forward swing by the lateral shift, some of the weight will have moved to the outside of your left heel.

4. Did your head remain still? If so, it will be in the same position as in the original setup.

5. Is the straight-line relationship between the back of your left hand, your left arm, and the shaft of the club unchanged? Avoid any inward cupping of the left hand and wrist at impact in an effort to get the ball into the air. This is sometimes called "scissoring," which is caused by the clubhead's getting ahead of the hands before the ball is hit. This inward cupping breaks the straight line between the left forearm and hand, which in turn shortens the arc of the swing. As a result, the ball will be "sculled" (that is, hit too low) or topped along the

The straight-line relationship between the back of your left hand, left arm, and the shaft of the club must remain unchanged at the end of the mini forward swing.

On the mini forward swing, avoid any inward cupping of the left hand and wrist at impact. This is sometimes called "scissoring" and is caused by the clubhead getting ahead of the hands before the ball is hit. Scissoring breaks the straight line between the left forearm and hand, which in turn shortens the arc of the swing.

ground. Scissoring may also be responsible for increasing the effective loft of the club. In that instance, the ball flies higher than it should and thereby loses distance. Imagine that your left hand and forearm are bound in a splint and move them together as one without a break.

When I started playing golf, I was convinced that I could generate greater clubhead speed and hit the ball farther by swinging my arms fast. The faster the arms swung, the faster the club would move—or so I thought. Older and more experienced players disagreed, and, fortunately, those wiser heads prevailed. I soon learned that the faster I tried to swing the club, the less distance I was getting. The speed of my arms was causing a premature action of my hands on the downswing with a loss of clubhead speed. My arms were swinging fast, but the club was swinging slowly.

Even an experienced golfer should go back to the miniswing once in a while and practice it. It is always valuable to begin practice sessions by hitting a few balls with a miniswing. It helps seasoned players as well as beginners to make sure that the body is moving in the proper direction together with the arms and hands.

Learning to make a proper miniswing is one of the most important steps in learning a good full golf swing. Once you have learned to hit the ball in the right way with a miniswing, you will have learned the proper takeaway for a full swing and how the ball must be struck in the crucial hitting area of the full swing. Thus you will be well on your way toward building a sound, rewarding golf swing.

Remember, you are hitting only small shots in the miniswing, so do not try to swing fast or hard to hit the ball. Moving the hands or arms quickly or swinging hard makes it much more difficult to feel what you are trying to do. Avoid any attempt for distance at this stage. No one can hit the ball far with a miniswing anyway, so take it easy.

LENGTHENING THE MINI FORWARD SWING INTO THE FULL FOLLOW-THROUGH

In Lesson Three you learned the miniswing—what it is, how to execute it, and, finally, how to hit the ball with it. The miniswing is a learning aid of such importance that it should be mastered before tackling the full swing.

The mini backswing is the first movement you will make in the full backswing, and the movement of the lower body that you made at the start of the mini forward swing is also the first movement of the full downswing.

The miniswing has proved to be an exceptionally effective base on which to build a sound golf swing. In actual play it is lengthened in order to generate enough power to hit the ball the necessary distance.

In a well-executed swing, the player's body coils as he swings the club with his hands and arms into a full backswing. Clubhead speed is produced by the uncoiling of the body as the club swings down to hit the ball and passes beyond the hitting area into a full follow-through. (For the follow-through, see Lesson Five.)

In most methods of instruction, the student is expected to learn the backswing, downswing, and follow-through all at the same time in actual swings. Although this is logical, I have found with the GSM that it is more effective in the early learning or relearning process to have the student extend the mini forward swing into a full follow-through before extending the mini backswing into a full backswing. (Of course, in actual play, when making short shots the swing is approximately the same length on the forward swing as on the backswing.)

Using only a mini backswing makes it easier for you to concentrate on making the correct forward swing and follow-through and knowing how that swing looks and feels. From a full backswing position, the downswing happens too quickly for you to feel the direction in which you are swinging the club. Therefore, the very lack of clubhead speed in the miniswing becomes an advantage. I am sure you would find that a longer backswing at this time would make it much more difficult to learn the proper full follow-through.

If you have mastered the miniswing and can execute it with consistency, you will find the follow-through relatively easy.

In this lesson of the GSM, the full follow-through will be undertaken in two steps. First you will extend the mini forward swing to a position where your arms and hands and the shaft of the club are at hip level (Checkpoint 1). Then you will continue the swing from that point into a full follow-through (Checkpoint 2).

How do you know you are in the correct position? Hold each position and, after a pause, look at it. Note what it looks like and feels like. Again, your mirror, along with the checkpoints, will help to guide you.

THE PARTIAL FOLLOW-THROUGH

Grip the club, set up to an imaginary ball, and make the miniswing as described in Lesson Three. If you check your position at the end of the swing, you will notice that your body is still facing to the front, with the shoulder line still parallel to the target line. Your left arm, the back of your left hand, and the shaft of the club will still form a straight line, unbroken by any bending of your wrist or elbow. Some of your weight will have shifted to the outside of your left heel.

Repeat the miniswing, but this time lengthen the follow-through by pushing the balls of your feet against the ground, as your legs continue their lateral motion far enough so that they start to turn out of the way to the left of the target line.

This continuing lateral movement of your legs should pull your right knee in toward the left leg, with the right heel coming off the ground. That takes most of the weight off your right foot and transfers it to the outside of the left heel. Although your head stays in the same position as it was at the start, the right shoulder continues to move down and underneath the chin as the right arm straightens and passes over the left. This is the first point in the forward swing at which the clubhead moves ahead of the hands. The turning motion of your body will cause the clubhead to come inside the target line.

At this halfway point, Checkpoint 1, both arms should be straight. Your right arm, the back of your right hand, and the shaft of the club should form a straight line parallel to the target line. The toe of the clubhead should now point toward the sky. The relation between your right arm and the shaft of the club as they extend parallel to the target line is one of the best ways to check your swing at this position in the follow-

To begin the partial follow-through, grip the club, set up to an imaginary ball, and make the miniswing. Your body should still be facing front with the shoulder line parallel to the target line.

Lengthen the swing by pushing the balls of your feet against the ground, as your legs continue their lateral motion far enough so that they start to turn out of the way to the left of the target line.

through. As a final check, be sure that your head has not shifted from its original setup position. If you study photos of professional golfers at this point in the swing, you will notice that their eyes seem to be riveted on the spot where the ball was and their heads have not moved.

Practice this partial follow-through in front of your mirror, and check each time that you are doing it properly. If you end up consistently in the correct finish position, you are ready to start hitting balls.

It will take only a few shots with this partial follow-through to determine whether or not you are getting the ball up into the air and hitting it straight. If you are not, review Lesson Three on the miniswing.

Checkpoint 1

This continuing lateral movement of your legs should pull your right knee in toward the left leg, with the right heel coming off the ground. Although your head stays in the same position as it was in at the start, the right shoulder continues to move down and underneath the chin while the right arm straightens and passes over the left.

At this halfway checkpoint in the follow-through, Checkpoint 1, both arms should be straight. Your right arm, the back of your right hand, and the shaft of the club should form a straight line parallel to the target line. The toe of the clubhead should now point toward the sky.

Remember, lifting the arms and clubhead abruptly upward as the ball is hit can cause topped or sculled shots. Many of the early instructors put it this way: "If you want the ball to get up, hit it down. Try to lift it up, it'll stay down." Simple but true. In order to get the ball off the ground, you must keep the clubhead low. This allows the clubhead to strike the bottommost part of the ball at impact. All golf clubs are designed in such a way that the angle (or loft) of the clubface will get the ball into the air. The more loft on the club—for instance, the shorter irons (6, 7, 8, 9, wedge)—the higher and shorter the distance the ball will travel. The less-lofted, longer-shafted clubs (2, 3, 4, and 5 irons and the woods) will hit the ball lower in the air and farther.

Do not attempt or expect to hit these balls far or very high in the air. No one can hit the ball any appreciable distance from a mini backswing. The important things to find out are, first, is the ball getting up into the air and going straight, and, second, are you in the correct finish position. Your honest answers will be the true test of your progress.

CHECKPOINT 2

THE FINISH POSITION

Once you are able to hit balls accurately with a partially extended follow-through, you are ready to extend the swing into a full follow-through.

At Checkpoint 1, the halfway or hip-level checkpoint, both arms are fully extended and straight. Your right arm, the back of your right hand, and the shaft of your club form a straight line parallel to the target line.

First let me give you a brief preview of what will happen when the swing is lengthened from hip level to a full follow-through.

To reach the correct finish position from Checkpoint 1, the left side of your body will continue to turn away from the target line. Your arms will continue their upward motion accompanied by a gradual bending of the hands at the wrists. In this way the shaft of the club will be swung up to its finish position between the left shoulder and your head. But before you can do this, you must know the function of the hands and arms. Until now, there has been no wrist action in the swings you have made; that is, the hands have not bent at the wrists.

A Helpful Exercise

Here is a simple exercise to help you understand how the hands should bend at the wrists. Grip the club and hold it out in front of you with both arms fully extended and the shaft parallel to the ground. Without moving your arms at all, bend your hands upward toward the center of your forehead. If the grip is flexible (as it should be), you will be able to do this easily without any loosening of the fingers on the club.

This particular movement of the hands in relation to your forearms is called hinging the wrists. (In the backswing, it is frequently called cocking the wrists.) Practice this exercise a few times.

Now, from the Checkpoint 1 position, let your arms continue their upward motion as your hands and wrists hinge toward a position between your head and left shoulder. Even though your right arm remains relatively straight, this hinging will cause your left arm to bend at the elbow and point to the ground at the completion of your follow-through.

As this hinging of your wrists and the bending of the left arm take place, your head should gradually come up, too. Holding the head down too long may restrict a complete, fluid follow-through. The right side of your body will be tilted down and lower than the left. This will place the body in a graceful finish position, with your back arched in the shape of a reverse C. Most of the weight of your lower body will have shifted from the right foot to the outside of the left heel. Your right knee and toe should be pointing in a direction parallel to the target line.

A helpful way to tell whether you have shifted your weight sufficiently to the left leg and foot at the finish of the

A simple exercise to understand how the hands should bend at the wrists in the follow-through begins by gripping the club and holding it out in front of you with both arms fully extended and the shaft parallel to the ground.

Without moving your arms at all, bend your hands upward toward the center of your forehead. This movement is called "hinging the wrists."

In the backswing, hinging the wrists, shown here from the front, is frequently called "cocking the wrists."

The full follow-through begins at Checkpoint 1, or the partial follow-through. At Checkpoint 1 both arms are fully extended and straight. Your right arm, the back of your right hand, and the shaft of your club form a straight line parallel to the target line.

From Checkpoint 1 let your arms continue their upward motion as your hands and wrists hinge toward a position between your head and left shoulder.

swing is to see if you can lift your right foot and still maintain your balance. If most of your weight has been shifted properly, it should be easy to do. Look at photos of good golfers; you will sometimes see a few spikes on the instep side of their left shoe at the finish of the swing. This indicates that the weight has been transferred fully to the outside of the left foot.

Now try hitting some balls with the short mini back-

As the hinging of your wrists and the bending of the left arm occur, your head should gradually come up too. Holding the head down too long may restrict a complete, fluid follow-through.

At the finish of the follow-through, the right side of the body will be tilted down and lower than the left. This will place the body in a graceful finish position, with your back arched in the shape of a reverse C. Most of the weight of your lower body will have shifted from the right foot to the outside of your left heel. Your right knee and toe should be pointing in a direction parallel to the target line.

swing, extending the forward miniswing into a full follow-through. A full follow-through from such a short backswing may feel restricted and stiff at first, but try not to compensate for it by swinging the club fast. Remember that from a mini backswing with no wrist action you will generate very little momentum to help complete the follow-through. Therefore, the clubhead will not have sufficient speed to propel the ball very far. Don't expect distance; that will come later.

Checkpoint 1, the partial follow-through, seen from the left side.

The hands and wrists hinge as you let your arms continue their upward motion from Checkpoint 1.

In fact, the lack of clubhead speed and the deliberate swing help you to feel your body, together with your hands and arms, moving correctly into the full follow-through. It is a practice swing with a golf ball. Hence, your concentration

The head should gradually come up as you hinge your wrists and bend the left arm.

At Checkpoint 2, the full follow-through, the right side of the body will be tilted down and lower than the left.

should be on making the proper swing and on what that swing looks and feels like. At this point, the shape of the swing is your primary concern.

THE BACKSWING

Your golf swing at this stage could be aptly compared to a well-made car with one thing missing—a sufficiently powerful engine. A car, no matter how finely constructed, cannot move efficiently without enough power. Neither can the golfer hit a ball far unless he generates the necessary power by swinging the club from a full backswing. In fact, the purpose of the backswing is to put the club into a position from which it can be swung squarely into the back of the ball with maximum speed. In short, the purpose of the full backswing is to hit the ball farther.

Lengthening the backswing will be your goal in this lesson. To accomplish this we shall apply the same method used in learning the full follow-through. Establishing two separate checkpoints will make it easier for you to learn the full backswing. First, you will extend the mini backswing to a halfway or hip-level position (Checkpoint 3), and, second, you will swing beyond that checkpoint into the full backswing position (Checkpoint 4).

Before starting to build the full backswing, study the illustrations on pages 72–73. They will show you clearly what a good backswing looks like.

Next let's review what you have accomplished so far. You will remember that you initiated the mini backswing by pushing the clubhead straight back from the ball with an extended left arm. That moved the clubhead back 12 inches from the ball and low to the ground. As the clubhead moved back, the beginning of the shoulder turn started to bring the clubhead inside the target line. There was no wrist action in the mini backswing, and no attempt was made to start the club back with the arms and hands moving independently of the shoulders. In the mini backswing, your arms and hands maintained their original positions relative to your chest. Throughout this mini movement your head remained motionless.

From the mini backswing you were able to hit the ball straight but not far. Now you are ready to lengthen the mini backswing by extending it to the first checkpoint in the backswing—Checkpoint 3 in the full swing.

CHECKPOINT 3

THE PARTIAL BACKSWING

First be sure that your grip is correct and that you are setting up to the ball properly. The clubhead should be placed behind the ball, square to the target line and with the imaginary lines across your shoulders, hips, knees, and toes, respectively, parallel to that line. The back of the ball is positioned on an imaginary line extending perpendicular to the target line from a point midway between your heels. Your hands should be slightly ahead of the ball, with the left arm, the back of the left hand, and the shaft of the club forming a straight line. Your weight should be between the balls of your feet and the heels, slightly on the inside of the feet and evenly divided between them. Your back should be straight, and you should be bending forward from the waist. The knees are flexed a little and in a slightly knock-kneed position.

Now make a mini backswing—but this time continue pushing the clubhead farther back from the ball, with a fully extended left arm. As a result of your left shoulder's continuing to turn and tilt, you will begin to feel the big muscles of your left side also beginning to turn and stretch. The turn and tilt of your shoulders will help to bring the club gradually upward until your arms and hands reach a position that is approximately waist high. This is Checkpoint 3, the first half of your backswing.

At this checkpoint, your left arm, the back of your left hand, and the shaft of the club should form a straight line parallel to the target line and to the ground. There is no wrist action up to this point in the backswing. The toe of the club should point to the sky if you have retained the correct square clubface established in the setup position. Since you were bending from the waist in the setup, your shoulders will have continued to tilt as well as turn as the club was swung back. Thus, the left shoulder is now lower than the right. This checkpoint is very important—it will help you know whether or not you have started the club back correctly.

Here again you can check yourself in the mirror. Notice that this position is almost the exact counterpart of Checkpoint 1, your position at the halfway point in the full follow-through, left and right being reversed. You will notice too that as an automatic result of your shoulders having made a fuller turn in this longer backswing, your upper torso and left hip will have also begun to turn. As your left hip begins to turn, the left knee will start to point toward the ball, shifting some more of your weight to the inside of your right foot and leg.

If your backswing at Checkpoint 3 differs from the position described before, go back and try again. An error at this critical stage will inevitably compound itself if you fail to correct it before continuing on to the full backswing.

For example, if the club is lifted abruptly by your hands and arms, you will have failed to give your upper body a

To begin the partial backswing, be sure that your grip is correct and that you are setting up to the ball properly. Make a mini backswing.

Continue the mini backswing by pushing the club-head farther back from the ball, with a fully extended left arm.

chance to turn as well as tilt into a full tight backswing. That will prevent you from making a powerful downswing. Also, it is difficult to swing the club back in the proper direction with consistency if your arms and hands are not moving together with the upper body. The first half of the backswing must be a single, coordinated movement.

An excellent way to help you develop the feel of keeping the clubhead low to the ground is to practice with a weighted club. Small weights are available that can be easily attached to the clubhead, or you can use a weighted headcover. Using a weighted clubhead will help you learn how to achieve a good, low takeaway while keeping the club down longer.

After a few practice swings have helped you acquire the

As a result of your left shoulder's continuing to turn and tilt, you will begin to feel the big muscles of your left side also beginning to turn and stretch.

The turn and tilt of your shoulders will help to bring the club gradually upward until your arms and hands reach a position that is approximately waist high. This is Checkpoint 3, at which your left arm, the back of your left hand, and the shaft of the club should form a straight line parallel to the target line and the ground. The toe of the club should point toward the sky.

feel of this longer backswing, try hitting some balls. You may find that increasing the length of the backswing beyond a short miniswing has made it more difficult to hit the ball straight. This is to be expected, because your attention must now be divided between making a longer backswing, then making a correct downswing and follow-through. In fact, you may feel that though your swing has lengthened your progress has been slowed—perhaps even regressed. This is natural, but only temporary. Don't be discouraged, since with practice and concentration your confidence will grow and soon you will successfully combine this longer backswing with all you have accomplished before.

CHECKPOINT 4

THE FULL BACKSWING

Now that you have learned how to extend the mini backswing to a halfway checkpoint in which your left arm, the back of your left hand, and the shaft of the club end up approximately waist high and parallel to the target line, we can now proceed to Checkpoint 4, the full backswing.

The full backswing is a further lengthening of this half backswing. Just as the miniswing provides a checkpoint for the first 12 inches or so of the backswing, the half backswing provides another important checkpoint. Remember that the positions of your body, arms, and club at the mini and half backswings are identical to their positions in the full backswing.

Let us now continue the backswing from this halfway checkpoint to the full backswing position—Checkpoint 4 and your final checkpoint.

Set up to an imaginary ball, making sure of a good grip, a square clubface, and the proper posture. Take the club back to the halfway checkpoint and continue turning the shoulders and upper left side of your body as your hands and wrists hinge the clubshaft upward in a direction parallel to the target line. The arms should continue their upward motion until the club reaches a position well above the right shoulder.

Be sure that the straight-line relation between the back of your left hand, wrist, and lower forearm is maintained. The left shoulder should be under or slightly past your chin. Even though your hands and wrists hinge, the left arm should remain straight, but not rigid or stiff. Your right arm, which was slightly flexed at the setup, should now bend in such a way that your elbow points to the ground.

Throughout the backswing, your head must remain steady. It is the hub of the golf swing around which your body turns.

The full rotation of your upper body at the completion of the backswing will have caused your hips to turn about half as much as the shoulders. This increased rotation of the hips pulls the left knee into a position pointing at or slightly to the right of the ball.

To accomplish this full turn, your left heel may come off the ground a little. This is perfectly permissible.

The right knee remains flexed as in the original setup position, and some more of your weight will now have shifted over to the inside of your right foot and leg. Be very careful that your left knee does not move forward (toward the target line) as the club is swung into a full backswing. Should that happen, it will keep too much weight on your left foot and leg and prevent the proper weight shift.

Let us return for a moment to the clubshaft itself at the top of the backswing. It should be parallel to the target line. This is an important fundamental. In the case of the longer wood clubs, the shaft may be swung farther back so that it is also parallel to the ground. However, with all clubs on full swings, the clubshaft should always be parallel to the target line. Here again your mirror will show you the accuracy of your backswing and help you determine what the proper position should be.

Since the correct hinging (or cocking) of the hands and wrists upward on the backswing is of such importance, the simple exercise prescribed in the full follow-through is equally helpful here (see Lesson Four).

Grip the club, and hold your arms and the club straight out in front of you. Now, without moving your arms, hinge the hands and wrists upward toward the center of your forehead. This is the proper movement of the hands, relative to your forearms, as your wrists hinge on the backswing.

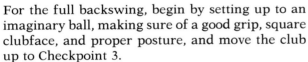

For the full backswing, begin by setting up to an imaginary ball, making sure of a good grip, square clubface, and proper posture, and move the club up to Checkpoint 3.

Continue turning your shoulders and upper left side as your hands and wrist hinge the clubshaft upward. The arms should continue their upward motion until the club reaches a position well above the right shoulder.

Now repeat the full backswing several times. The following checklist of questions will be valuable as you study your position at the completion of the full backswing.

1. Did you turn your left shoulder under or slightly past your chin? If not, your backswing may very well have been a "false" one. That is, it was made only with the arms and hands without the proper turning of the upper body. A false backswing will prevent appreciable club-head speed in the downswing and cause a considerable

Be sure that the straight-line relationship between the back of your left hand, wrist, and lower forearm is maintained. The left shoulder should be under or slightly past your chin.

In the full backswing, Checkpoint 4, the left arm should remain straight. Your right arm, which was slightly flexed at the setup, should now bend in such a way that your elbow points to the ground. The full rotation of your upper body at the finish of the backswing will have caused your hips to turn about half as much as the shoulders.

loss of distance. Also, without the full shoulder turn the club may very well be swung in the wrong direction on the downswing.

2. Did you keep your head steady?

3. Did your hips turn only half as much as your shoulders? If they turned too far you cannot achieve a tightly wound backswing.

4. Did your left knee point at or behind the ball? Did the right knee remain flexed as some of your weight shifted to the inside of your right foot and leg?

5. As your body coiled, did your hands and wrists at approximately hip level start to hinge upward in a direction parallel to the target line as the clubshaft was swung well above your right shoulder?

6. Did you keep the straight-line relation between the back of your left hand, wrist, and lower forearm?

7. Was the clubshaft in a position parallel to the target line? If it pointed to the right of the target line, it was "across the line"; if it pointed to the left of the line, it was "laid off." Both extremes should be avoided, because either one will usually make it difficult to swing the club accurately into and along the target line.

8. Was the left arm straight, and did the right elbow point downward?

You should spend as much time as possible practicing the backswing, until it feels natural to swing the club into the correct position at the top as your upper body coils tightly.

Be sure to look at your positions at both Checkpoint 3 and Checkpoint 4 as you work on the backswing. Knowing what the correct shape looks like will make it easier for you to get the feel for the proper backswing. That feel is the basis for consistency and a "grooved" swing.

MAKING THE FULL SWING

In this lesson you will bring together all you have learned in Lessons One through Five using the Graduated Swing Method. At the end of this lesson you will be hitting balls from a full swing.

You already know how to wind your body into a tightly coiled backswing and how to swing the club into its proper position at the top of the backswing. You also know how the clubface must make square contact with the ball along the target line and how the club should be swung into the complete follow-through. The only thing that remains to be learned is how to swing the club down into the hitting area from the full backswing.

THE DOWNSWING

First I want to give you a brief preview of what happens on the downswing of a full swing. Your backswing has put you into the ideal position from which to hit the ball straight and as far as necessary in actual play. As the body unwinds or uncoils, the hands and arms swing the club down in approximately the same path in which it was taken back. This means that from a full backswing the club swings from inside the target line to strike the ball and momentarily moves along that line after impact. The continuing body turn brings the club back inside the target line and into a full follow-through.

Power on the downswing is generated when the thrusting of the legs keys or pulls the upper body down into the hitting area. The legs, by their lateral movement, in effect set up a muscular chain reaction. That is, the legs pull the hips around, the hips transfer the pulling to the upper body and shoulders, the arms and hands pick it up from the shoulders, and the hands in turn pass the energy along through the shaft to the clubhead. This release of power reaches the clubhead through the wrists as they uncock to swing the club freely to hit the ball.

Swinging in the proper sequence on the downswing produces clubhead speed and thus distance. When Julius Boros was active on the pro tour he was famous for his "easy" swing. Because he coordinated the motions of his arms and hands with the movement of his body to time the release of the club perfectly he was able to generate tremendous clubhead speed in a seemingly effortless manner. A number of women professionals also provide excellent examples of the power that can be generated. Many of the women pros are small and light, yet some of them can hit the ball 240 yards or more.

Now that you know the proper path of the club in a good downswing, the next portion of Lesson Six will cover learning how to swing it on that path.

One of the advantages of the GSM is that all of your practicing will now pay off as you prepare to put it all together and hit the ball from a fully wound backswing. The lateral movement of the lower body (the legs) that you used to initiate the forward swing from both the mini backswing and the partial backswing is the same movement you will make to start your downswing from the full backswing. The only difference is that in the full backswing that movement is more pronounced. The direction in which your legs start to move will vary because of a bigger shoulder and hip turn, but the basic lateral thrusting of the legs in the direction your hips are pointing remains the same.

If when you put yourself in a proper full backswing your feeling is "where do I go from here?," remember that you have made the proper lower body move before and all you have to do is repeat it.

A Helpful Exercise

Just as the exercise in which you placed your hands on the sides of your upper legs helped you get the feel of the initial move that starts the mini forward swing, here is another exercise that will help you learn what really happens when you start the downswing from a full backswing position.

Take your club and make a full backswing as described in Lesson Five. Hold it there and check yourself in the mirror for the proper position. Now, while still looking in the mirror, push with the balls of your feet and move your knees sideways to the left. Done properly, this action of the lower body will start to move the right shoulder and the arms downward. In the earlier miniswing exercise, the shoulders and arms moved with the legs as they thrust sideways. The same thing is happening now, but from a full backswing position. Your right elbow stays close to your side as the right shoulder tilts down. Take the club up to the top again and repeat the exercise a few times, watching yourself in the mirror. It will help you feel what should be happening as you start the downswing from a full backswing position.

Once again, the key is that the feet and legs should activate the movement of the shoulders and the arms.

To learn what happens in the downswing, take your club and make a full backswing. Hold it there and check yourself in the mirror for the proper position.

Next, push with the balls of your feet and move your knees sideways to the left.

Done properly, this action of the lower body will start to move the right shoulder and the arms downward. Your right elbow stays close to your side as the right shoulder tilts down.

THE FULL SWING

Repeat the full swing (with an imaginary ball) several times, and swing the club into a full follow-through. These practice swings will also help you feel what the full golf swing is like. Many of my students claim that they can make a near-perfect practice swing without a ball. But as soon as the ball is there, the coordination seems to disappear. The practice swing was probably in error, too, but because a ball was not there to be hit incorrectly, they felt that the execution was perfect. Don't be careless with these rehearsal swings, or you may make the same mistakes in your swing with the ball that you made in the practice swing.

Remember that you start the downswing with the lateral thrusting motion of the legs that you used to start the mini forward swing and the forward swing from Lesson Four's Checkpoint 3 (the partial follow-through). But now, because your hips have turned more as a result of a full shoulder turn, even though the leg movement is the same, the direction is diagonal to instead of parallel to the target line.

Be sure that your arms and hands follow the movement of the lower body, swinging the club into and along the target line. Most of your weight will shift over onto the left leg as you continue into your full follow-through, with the right shoulder ending up lower than the left and the clubshaft finishing between the head and left shoulder.

Before starting to hit balls with a full swing, use the photos on pages 85–91 as a review of your progress to this point. It may also be helpful to refer back occasionally to a given lesson and reread the pertinent section or sections.

Also before trying to hit balls with the full swing, it would be prudent first to work your way up to a full swing in logical stages.

Before starting to hit balls with a full swing, use the photographs on pages 85–91 as a review of your progress to this point. Begin with the proper setup position and grip.

The mini backswing.

Checkpoint 3, the half backswing.

Checkpoint 4, the full backswing.

(A) The downswing.

(B)

(C)

(D)

The mini forward swing.

Checkpoint 1, the partial follow-through.

Checkpoint 2, the full follow-through.

Grip your club, set it down behind the ball with a square clubface, and assume the proper square setup position. For the first few swings use only the mini backswing, but continue the swing into a full follow-through. It is important that you examine your grip before and after each shot to be sure that it is correct. Also, continually check for a square clubface. Now extend the backswing to Checkpoint 3, the halfway point. Remember to push the clubhead straight back, low to the ground, with an extended left arm and let the turn and tilt of the left shoulder bring the club upward until you reach the waist-level halfway checkpoint. Make sure that the left arm, the back of your left hand, and the clubshaft form a straight line parallel to the target line, with the toe of the club pointing up. Each time, continue the downswing into a full follow-through.

Continue hitting balls, but now extend the backswing into a fully wound position. Remember on the full backswing that as your hands and arms swing the clubshaft upward, well above the right shoulder, your left shoulder turns underneath your chin. Your left arm remains straight; the right arm is bent with the elbow pointing toward the ground. As a result of your upper body making a full turn, the hips will turn half as much as your shoulders. This causes additional weight to shift to the inside of the right foot. Throughout, the head remains steady.

Now initiate the downswing in exactly the same manner that you used in your practice swings.

When hitting balls in the full swing, avoid trying to guide the clubhead. By the same token, don't hit "at" the ball either, but keep the club swinging through the ball right up into your full finish. Make the swing a complete, single unit, pretending that the ball just happens to be in the way.

In working to build or to improve a golf swing, there is always the danger of becoming so involved with various details that one loses sight of the necessary final goal—swinging the club. Of course, proper technique is essential, but all of this is directed toward making square, solid contact with the ball as the club is swung in the right direction. After all, the ball is not struck with the body, the legs, the arms, or the hands; it is propelled by the clubhead only. The swinging motion of the club should integrate all the movements of the body.

USING DIFFERENT CLUBS

After a few practice sessions, if you are reasonably satisfied with your progress hitting balls with the full swing off the tee, place the ball on an artificial grass mat or a level lie on the turf. After you hit quite a few shots off the turf with your 9 iron, gradually work your way up through the other short irons, the middle irons, the long irons, and finally the woods. Make sure that with each club you are hitting the ball well enough to move on to the next club.

Remember also that as you move up from the 5 iron into the long irons and woods, your stance should widen somewhat for better balance, and the ball placement should change from the center of your feet to approximately 2 inches to the right of the left heel.

You may find that each time you add different clubs in your practice, or move the ball from the tee to the turf, you are not able to hit the ball quite as well as you did previously. But stay with it; make whatever corrections are called for and continue hitting balls.

As you move along in your practice sessions, change clubs frequently. Try to keep every full swing the same, no matter what club you may be using. Don't attempt to gain distance by hitting hard; that will only compound the difficulty of being able to feel the correct swing.

Try to concentrate on the proper shape and direction of the swing as you make it, and do not allow yourself to get upset over poorly hit shots. You will have your share of them; everyone does. Even the great Walter Hagen during his prime in competition once remarked that he would "miss" six or seven shots in every round he played. Accepting the fact that some shots would be missed helped him to remain calm when the inevitable bad shots occurred. This attitude is good for all of us to develop. Get your satisfaction from your good shots, and concentrate on increasing the percentage of those. Enjoy hitting balls; make practice sessions a time to look forward to.

If you find that you are having a specific problem that cannot be answered by going back to Lesson One through Six, you may well find the answer in the last chapter, "Questions Most Frequently Asked."

TODAY'S GOLF SWING

For a better understanding of the modern golf swing, it is instructive to compare it with the swing that was used in the past and to trace some of the improvements in technique that have been made over the years. We can do this by studying photographs of some of the early players in action.

Our golfing ancestors used to swing the club around their bodies in a flatter swingplane than is standard today. Their characteristically "roundhouse" swing made it far more difficult for them to hit straight shots consistently, because the clubhead stayed on the target line for a relatively short time.

There were various reasons why the swing of earlier eras was flatter. Compared with today's setup standards, the players stood much straighter to the ball, with very little bend from the waist. As a result their shoulders tilted a great deal less as they turned. Their equipment, too, made a difference. The whippy hickory shafts they used made it necessary to manipulate the club with the hands to get the clubface square as they hit the ball. The environment was a factor, too. They played primarily on the windswept courses of Scotland and England, so they learned to keep the ball low to cut down the effect of the wind.

Of course, all the great players of the past were still able to manipulate the club effectively with their hands in order to hit the ball into a desired position on the fairway or green. But they usually did that by "drawing" the ball from right to left in a rather low trajectory.

The more upright modern swing brought with it several marked advantages. The clubhead stays longer on the target line when the ball is hit, thus increasing the chances of hitting the ball straighter and higher. And, since iron shots come onto the green from a higher trajectory, they have more consistent stopping action ("bite"), permitting the player to hit the ball up closer to the hole on the first bounce.

Do not infer from these comments that I subscribe to the notion that everything old is bad, all that is new good; far from it. Sound fundamentals from our golfing forebears have been retained, improved, and combined with innovations of the modern era and resulted in the most successful golf swing to this day.

There are exceptions, of course, in every period. I was reminded of that recently when I came across some photographs of Jim Barnes, a great player of the 1920s—a U.S. Open champion and winner of the first PGA tournament. Compared with his contemporaries, "Long Jim" had a more upright swing pattern. Whether this was done by intent or by chance we will never know, but it is clear from the photos that he swung the club much like the fine players who followed him with the "modern" swing. I'm sure that swing accounts to a large degree for the success he enjoyed during his years of competitive play.

In the case of Byron Nelson, who in the 1930s became the father of the modern swing, there is no doubt that the improvements he introduced were brought about by intent. Nelson knew he was modernizing the swing and why. His results are evidenced by the phenomenal records he compiled in every category of tournament play.

Nelson's swing was simpler; it utilized the large muscles of the body more effectively, and it was upright. His pronounced bend from the waist improved his setup position and allowed his shoulders to tilt to a greater degree when they turned. This, together with the upward hinging of the hands and wrists, kept the club more upright on the backswing instead of more around the body, which was formerly practiced. Overall, these modifications produced a more upright swing. By combining this improvement in the backswing with a pronounced lateral thrust of his legs to initiate the downswing, Nelson achieved a sounder swing because the clubhead swung into and stayed on the target line longer as the ball was hit. As a result, "Lord" Byron consistently produced longer and straighter shots. His technique had remarkable longevity, and countless great players right up to the present are still emulating him.

During the summer of 1957 I worked as an assistant at the Scioto Country Club in Columbus, Ohio. The head professional at that time was Jack Grout, a fine instructor highly regarded for his teaching. One day, while standing in the doorway of the golf shop looking out toward the first tee, I saw a young man wearing Bermuda shorts preparing to tee off. Until then all the good golf swings I had seen were relatively flat, the club being swung more around the body. This youngster in shorts and with a football player's physique brought the club considerably upward, almost to the point (it seemed to me then) that it was being "picked up." Of course, it wasn't at all, and the resulting shot was ample proof that his backswing position was powerful and sound. When he hit the ball it went up and up, straight out, and landed almost out of sight.

I soon learned that the young man's name was Jack Nicklaus. He was only seventeen at the time, and the year before he had won the Ohio Open, shooting a 63 on the last round, in which he was paired with Sam Snead.

In the following days I got to know Nicklaus and was fortunate enough to play with him throughout the summer. I took advantage of those opportunities to study his swing carefully and soon became convinced that this was one of the best and most powerful swings I had ever seen. Basically, his swing's mechanics were simple and easy to repeat. He swung the club back much straighter than other players did and worked it up instead of around. Little did I know at the time that I was playing with a golfer destined for superstardom, one whose swing would eventually become the reference standard for a whole generation of golfers.

Nicklaus practiced and played thousands of hours, as do all fine players, because, for the most part, the golf swing is learned by practicing and playing. Competent instruction should accompany practice and play; otherwise bad habits can become so ingrained that they are almost impossible to correct. In most cases, the more rounds a golfer plays, the more his playing ability will improve. The technique of striking the ball will become more polished, and a better knowledge of the myriad aspects of the game will have a chance to develop into a more confident approach. These aspects include such things as putting and short shots, club selection, distance judgment, a feeling for the turf and wind, how to play uphill, downhill, and sidehill lies, when to play safe and when to gamble, how to read greens, how to handle trouble shots, and, not least in importance, the general etiquette and courtesy of the game, which also adds to the pleasure of golf. Much of this can be learned by playing.

Even though Tom Watson, Nancy Lopez, or any number of other outstanding players can make golf look relatively easy, it is far from that. It is certainly one of the most difficult games ever devised, because, as already stated, the golf swing itself is unquestionably unnatural. A beginning golfer will find at first that many of the movements of the correct golf swing may make him feel downright uncomfortable. One reason this is so is that, unlike other sports, such as tennis or baseball, in golf the ball must be struck off the ground. A baseball player is free to swing at the ball anywhere from his knees to his shoulders. He also has the latitude of hitting the ball to right field, left field, or straightaway. The tennis player must be able to hit the ball when it is anywhere from just off the ground to high overhead, and he is free to return it to his opponent's right or left side, cross-court, down the line, over his opponent, directly at him, or low to his feet, using a forehand or backhand, holding the racquet with either hand or both.

Not so in golf. For every shot, the ball rests on the ground, at an odd angle to the golfer himself. It must be hit straight or he'll find himself in trouble. During a discussion between Sam Snead and a famous baseball player, the merits and degree of difficulty of the two games were argued. The "Slammer" capped it all by saying, "When you fellows hit a foul ball you get two more chances. When we hit one, we have to play it!"

Also, in most other sports, the participant is reacting to an opponent's move and placement of the ball. Therefore, the athlete's instinct relays immediately to his body what his movement should be. Again, it is far different in golf. The ball is always still; there is no chance to use an instinctive reaction. Because of this difference, there are many golfers who swear that the very stillness and innocent whiteness of a golf ball only adds to its intimidating challenge when one is faced with the job of striking it.

Ben Hogan once remarked that it was not that the average person cannot learn to play golf or improve his game, but it's just that he does not know what he's supposed to do. I certainly agree. Anyone with fairly good coordination, a sincere desire to learn, and a willingness to work can learn the game and derive proportionate pleasure from it.

I am hopeful that these pages have given you a clearer

insight into what you are "supposed to do." The Graduated Swing Method has been instrumental in accomplishing this for thousands of my students and has launched them on the right path toward understanding what they are supposed to do. I am confident that the GSM will prove equally effective for you.

Golf can be at once the most frustrating and most rewarding of games. Winston Churchill once commented: "Golf is a game in which you try to put a small ball into a small hole with implements singularly unsuited to the purpose." Even the ball itself can change in two little strokes from an ally to an enemy. In spite of all, a satisfying golf game can become the Holy Grail, ever to be sought. It is the seeking and the adventure of the quest that is important.

Harry Vardon, known primarily as the innovator of the overlapping grip, was a great champion prior to and after the turn of the century. He was a six-time winner of the British Open (1896–1914) and a winner of the U.S. Open (1900).

John H. Taylor, a contemporary of Harry Vardon, was also a player of extraordinary ability. He was the winner of the British Open in 1894, 1895, 1900, 1909, and 1913.

Jim Barnes was the U.S. Open champion in 1921. He was also the winner of the first PGA Tournament and is a member of the PGA Hall of Fame.

(A)   (B) (C)

(F)   (G) (H)

Byron Nelson, winner of countless tour events, including the U.S. Open in 1939, the 1940 and 1945 PGA championships, and the Masters in 1937 and 1942. In 1945 he was victorious in nineteen of the thirty tournaments that he entered. He is also a member of the PGA Hall of Fame. Photos *(A)*, *(B)*, and *(C)* show Nelson's waggle in preparation to starting the club back in photo *(D)*. Note his Checkpoint 3 position in photo *(E)*, his left arm and club shaft parallel to the target line.

(D)　(E)

(I)　(J)

(K)

(A)

(E) (B) (F)

(C) (D)

Sam Snead won the British Open once (1946), the Masters Tournament twice (1949 and 1954), and the PGA Championship three times (1942, 1949, and 1951). He is also a member of the PGA Hall of Fame. Notice in photo (B) Snead's left arm and club shaft are parallel to the target line—his Checkpoint 3 position.

(G)

(A)

(B)

Gary Player is a three-time winner of the Masters Tournament (1961, 1974, and 1978) and the British Open (1959, 1968, and 1974). He is also a two-time winner of the PGA Championship (1962 and 1972) and a winner of the U.S. Open (1965). Notice in photo *(E)* Player's straight-line relationship between his left arm, the back of his left hand, and the club shaft at impact and the position of his head behind the ball.

(E)

(F)

(C)

(D)

(G)

(H)

(A)

(B)
(E)

Tom Weiskopf won the British Open in 1973 and the Canadian Open in 1975. Weiskopf's golf swing is recognized as one of the best in the world.

(C)

(D)

(F)

(G)

(A)　　　　　　　(B)　　(C)

(G)　　　　　　　(H)　(I)

Jack Nicklaus, winner of nineteen major championships, is the greatest golfer of all time. Notice in photo (D) Nicklaus's Checkpoint 3, with his left arm and the club shaft parallel to the target line. In photo (I) his right arm and the club shaft are parallel to the target line— his Checkpoint 1. *Photos of Jack Nicklaus courtesy of Golf Digest Japan.*

(D) (E) (F)

(J) (K) (L)

QUESTIONS MOST FREQUENTLY ASKED

I wish it were possible for me to spend some time with each of you to help with any particular problem you may be having with your swing. The number of questions I have been asked about the golf swing over the years would fill several volumes; of course, lack of space makes it impossible to include all of them in this book. However, I have selected a few of the questions most frequently asked and hope that some of the answers will be helpful to you. Beyond that, your local professional will be happy to help you in any way he can.

Q. Why do I always slice the ball?
A. A slice, the ever-present enemy of most weekend or average golfers, is a ball that curves in the air to the right. If the curve is only slight, it is called a "fade." The ball can start to the left, go straight, or to the right, but in all cases it ends up to the right of its initial flight.

In a slice, the clubface is open to the intended line of flight at impact. The open clubface imparts left to right side spin, causing the ball to move in that direction. The degree to which the clubface is open will determine how violently the ball curves. Straightfaced, less-lofted clubs tend to slice the ball more severely, because they produce more sidespin. But it is certain that the arms and hands have failed to return the clubface to its original square position.

First, check your clubface alignment at the address position, making sure that it is square to the target line (the leading edge of the clubface perpendicular to the target line). Next, be sure that your grip is correct and that your hands are not positioned on the club too far to the left. (Remember, the line formed by the upper left thumb and forefinger should point to the right eye. The corresponding line of the right hand should also point to the right eye.) Even if the hands are positioned properly, they should not be too tight on the club. If they are, it may stop the swinging motion of the arms and hands on the downswing and prevent them from returning the clubface to its original square position. In your effort to eliminate the slice, it is imperative to have a square clubface at impact.

If your particular slice starts to the left and then curves to the right, you are swinging the club to the left of the target at impact instead of straight along the target line. This is called a "pull slice" and is one of the weakest shots in golf, because not only is the clubhead moving in the wrong direction, but it may approach the ball from too steep a downward angle and will make solid contact with the back of the ball difficult.

Whether your slice is the pull slice, the slice that starts out straight, or the one that starts right (the "push slice"), along with making sure that your setup position is parallel to the target line, be careful to swing the club forward *on* the target line as the ball is hit.

Carefully going over the preceding fundamentals and making the proper corrections should help you cure your slice.

Q. Why do I hit behind the ball?
A. There can be several reasons or a combination of reasons for hitting behind the ball. One of the most common is low-

ering the head or moving it to the right on the backswing. Another reason may be that your lower body is not initiating the downswing and shifting your weight over to the left leg. Uncocking the wrists very early on the downswing ("hitting from the top" or "casting") can also cause the same problem. There are other reasons, of course, but any of these mentioned may cause the clubhead to reach its low point in the swing and hit the ground before contacting the ball.

Be sure that your head remains steady, and that your lower body initiates the downswing, shifting your weight over to the left leg. This proper weight shift will help prevent a premature uncocking of the wrists.

Q. What is the swingplane?
A. The swingplane is the ideal track on which the arms and hands swing the club up and down. It is an imaginary flat surface that extends from the ball through the top of a golfer's right shoulder in a normal setup position. So the closer your club is swung in that plane, the more consistent your swing will be. (See the photos on pages 118–119.)

There are a few outstanding golfers today who are not "in plane" at the top of their backswings. But those with unorthodox swing patterns consistently manage to make the adjustments that get them back into a perfect position in the hitting area. They have been able to accomplish this because their sophisticated knowledge of the swing mechanics, mixed with continual practice, has given them a "grooved" swing. However, this is not recommended for the average player. If you strive instead to reach an "in plane" position, compensatory moves should not be necessary.

Through the years, golfers with the greatest swings and those whose swings have had considerable longevity have always been in their own proper swingplane. They include Bobby Jones, Byron Nelson, Harry Cooper, Sam Snead, Ben Hogan, Tommy Bolt, Julius Boros, Gene Littler, Gary Player, Tom Weiskopf, Johnny Miller, and Jack Nicklaus.

The swingplane is the ideal track on which the arms and hands swing the club up and down. It is an imaginary flat surface that extends from the ball through the top of a golfer's right shoulder in a normal setup position.

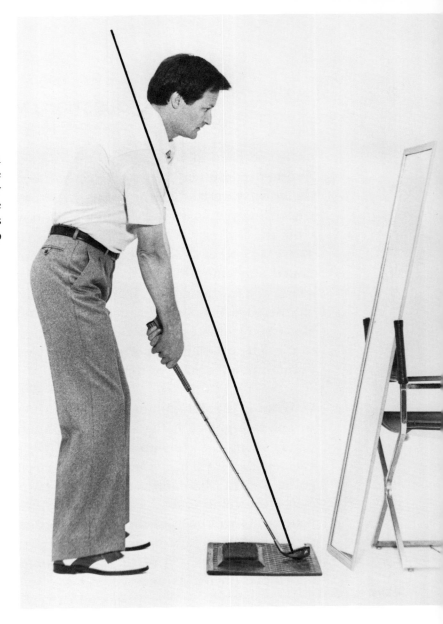

Q. Is the swingplane the same for all golfers?
A. No. There is no standard swingplane for all golfers. It is determined by the distance a player stands from the ball as he sets up to it. That distance itself is decided by the length of the particular club being used and the golfer's body build. In the following question, I comment on how the length of the club alters the swingplane, but for now we are concerned only with how a golfer's physique can affect that plane.

Strive to reach an "in plane" position as shown here. There are a few outstanding golfers today who are not "in plane" at the top of their backswings, but this is not recommended for the average player.

A golfer with relatively long arms as compared to his legs will of necessity stand farther from the ball and his swing will be flatter. The opposite body build, that is, a player with proportionately short arms and longer legs, will stand closer to the ball and his swing will be more upright. Tour players Lee Trevino and Tom Weiskopf are excellent examples of these respective swingplanes. But despite the marked differences in the two great golfers, both are swinging in their own plane.

Q. How do I know if my swing is in plane?
A. If you have followed the backswing checkpoints correctly you should be in your plane at the top of the backswing. However, since it is difficult at first to feel the proper position, there is a relatively easy way for you to find out. First ask a friend to stand facing your right shoulder along the target line. Now, with you in the setup position, have him close one eye and then align the shaft of the club between the ball and the top of your right shoulder. Be sure that he stands to your right along the target line. If at the top of your backswing your left arm and hand bisect the extension of that line, you are in your proper plane for that club.

Another dependable method of determining the accuracy of the swingplane is a videotape recorder with instant replay and stop action. At my golf studio in New York City, my machines are in constant use, because I have found them an excellent teaching aid to confirm easily and quickly whether or not our students are swinging in plane. Any guesswork or conjecture is eliminated, since the camera doesn't lie. As a rule, we take most of our footage with the TV camera shooting along the target line from the golfer's right as he sets up to the ball. On the glass screen of the monitor, we draw a grease-pencil line that runs from the ball through the top of the right shoulder and beyond. This line represents the correct swingplane for the particular club being used for the demonstration. Then, after the golfer has hit several shots, the swings are immediately replayed. On some, the action is stopped at the very top of the backswing. If at this point the swing is in plane, the left arm and hand will be on the plane line. The image on the monitor will also clearly reveal whether or not the clubshaft is parallel to the target line at the top of the backswing. Being able actually to see themselves helps our golfers swing the club up into this position more consistently at the completion of their backswings.

Starting with the shortest club, a wedge, and progressing to the driver, the longest one, the swing changes to a flatter plane, and the TV screen clearly shows the difference. When the golfer's club becomes longer, he stands farther from the ball and slightly straighter. The shoulders will tilt less when they turn, and as a result the swingplane becomes flatter. Although the angle of the swingplane does vary in this way from club to club, I continually emphasize that your feeling should be that you are trying to make precisely the same swing for all full shots.

Q. No matter how hard I try not to, I pull all of my shots. How can I correct this?
A. A "pull" is a straight shot to the left of the intended target. The club is swung in the wrong direction to the left, with the clubface square to this improper line at the moment of impact.

The first step toward correcting this problem is to check the plane of your backswing. Remember that to achieve a proper, in-plane backswing, you must start with a good setup position. Then, as the clubshaft swings up between your right shoulder and head and parallel to the target line, your left shoulder turns and tilts underneath your chin. Being properly in plane at the top of your backswing will make it easier for you to make the correct downswing consistently in the right direction.

In addition to making sure that the lower body initiates the downswing with the legs thrusting sideways, exaggerate keeping the clubhead, with the hands and arms, inside the target line until making contact with the ball. Don't be afraid of exaggerating any swing fundamental that you are learning. Many times it helps speed the process.

Q. What does "release the club" mean?
A. "Releasing the club" simply means that on a good downswing the arms and hands return the clubhead to its original square position. If the arms and hands fail to release the club, the clubface will be open at the moment of impact and the ball will be hit to the right.

Q. Why do I have to finish my swing? The ball is already gone.

A. The follow-through in a golf swing is a reflection of what preceded it. In a full swing, the club is moving so fast that any slowing or stopping of it prior to its reaching a complete finish has already started to happen before it ever struck the ball. The result is a loss of the clubhead speed that helps to carry you into a full finish.

Also, if your hands are too tight on the club, you may not be able to make a proper release on the downswing. Again, the swing then loses its momentum. Conversely, if the golfer releases the club too soon, the clubhead dissipates its acceleration before reaching the ball and robs the swing of its power.

A properly executed downswing, in which the club is swung freely, will invariably end in a fluid, complete follow-through. Therefore, a full finish is not an end in itself but rather the result of a good downswing.

Q. How do I _know_ if my clubface is square? I can't see it.

A. Fortunately, this is something you can check yourself by pausing in several different positions on a practice backswing and then looking directly at the clubhead or in a mirror. Of course, we are assuming that you are starting with the proper grip and a square clubface at the address position. You already know what that is: the leading edge of the club forming a perfect right angle to the target line. The straight-line relation between the back of your left hand, wrist, and lower forearm in the setup position should be maintained throughout the backswing.

After confirming that your clubface is square, the next check is the halfway point in the backswing. There the face of the club should be facing the target line and the toe pointing upward. Again on a practice swing, look at your clubhead upon the completion of a full backswing. If the clubface is facing the sky, it is "closed"; if the toe is pointing to the ground, the clubface is "open." The proper square clubface position is between the two extremes; that is, the clubface is half closed, with the toe of the club pointing partly down and partly out toward the target line.

It will become much easier for you to feel that the clubface is square once you know what it should look like. (See photo on page 19). You will then have a better opportunity of successfully keeping the clubface square throughout the entire swing.

Q. How can I stop "skying" my drives?
A. In most cases the ball will be hit too high (or "skied") when the plane of the backswing becomes excessively vertical or upright. The driver has been lifted abruptly on the backswing and brought down the same way in a chopping motion. This will cause the clubhead to contact the ball too far below its center. Many times you will strike the ground behind the ball at the same time.

To stop skied drives, be sure that you start the club back in one piece low to the ground. Your arms, with the turning of the upper body, can then bring the club more around you instead of straight upward. On the downswing this will help to keep the clubhead moving parallel to the ground just prior to, at, and immediately after contact with the ball. In other words, your driver should be swung low to the ground in the hitting area with a sweeping motion. This should end your "skied" drives.

Q. Why am I off balance when I finish my swing?
A. In all probability you are starting the downswing in the improper sequence. This may cause you to swing the club in the wrong direction. If your hands and arms start the downswing, the right shoulder tends to move out toward the target

line and the clubhead is swung from the outside across the target line to the left. The body weight then shifts from the balls of your feet to your toes, causing you to fall forward off balance. Starting the downswing in the correct sequence (feet, knees, and hips leading the upper body) helps to keep you in proper balance. In this way the upper body stays in position as the right shoulder tilts downward instead of moving out toward the target line. This will increase your chances of swinging the club from inside the target line and along it as the ball is hit. The clubhead should not cross the target line from inside out or outside in. Swinging the club in the proper sequence helps you to swing it in the right direction, which will in turn give you better balance at the finish of your swing.

Another balance fault in the finish is "going with the shot." That is, the head and body move forward with the club in the direction you are swinging it. This lunging motion is also caused by the upper body initiating the downswing instead of starting in the correct sequence—the lower body leading the upper, which keeps the upper in place. In this way, your back is curved in a modified reverse C position with the right shoulder tilted slightly below the left. This position should leave you well balanced.

Q. What is a waggle? Should I use one?
A. A "waggle" is simply small movements of the clubhead made with the hands and arms behind or over the ball as a golfer prepares to swing. Most good players employ some sort of waggle to help them prevent tightening up as they address the ball before initiating the actual swing. You too may find it helpful to incorporate a waggle into your setup just prior to starting the club back on the takeaway. Try it; if it works for you—use it.

Q. What causes me to shank my short pitch shots?
A. Short pitch shots are shanked for the same reasons any full

shot is shanked. It may be more common with the short shots because, of course, you are standing closer to the ball, which makes it easier for the clubhead to swing outside the ball. But in both cases the heel of the clubhead contacts the ball instead of the clubface, causing the ball to shoot off sharply to the right.

In all probability you are out of your swingplane on the backswing in an exaggerated way: far too vertical or too horizontal. Refer to Lesson Five for the proper halfway checkpoint position. Then, on the downswing, try to keep the clubhead inside the target line until you make contact with the ball. Keeping your right elbow close to your side will help to prevent the clubhead from swinging outside the ball.

Q. If the body moves one way on the backswing, why doesn't it move the same way in reverse on the downswing?
A. Even though that might simplify the swing, it just doesn't work that way. The natural movement of the hips and legs (as in baseball or tennis) would be an immediate rotation of the entire right side of the body coming around outside the left. The club could then be swung improperly outside the ball. But even if the clubhead stayed inside the target line as it should, the arc of the swing would be too circular and the club would stay on the target line too short a time. Unfortunately, this is often done. It is one of the most common faults in the swing. So, the longer the clubhead stays on the target line, the easier it is to hit straight shots consistently.

Properly, the legs should initiate the downswing by thrusting in a direction diagonal to the target line before the lower body turns out of the way. Then the upper body (shoulders, arms, and hands) is in position to swing the club into and along the target line to hit the ball.

This is further evidence that in golf the natural way is wrong in most cases.

Q. How can I stop bending my left arm when I make a full backswing?

A. It is important to maintain a straight left arm at the top of the backswing because without it the club is usually over-swung. This disallows a tight coiling of the upper body and may cause you to release the club prematurely on the downswing.

Remember to start the backswing by pushing the club-head straight back from the ball with a fully extended left arm so that it is not abruptly picked up by the right hand and arm (see Lesson Five). This will help ensure that the muscles of the upper left side dominate the swing and prevent the collapsing of the left arm.

Q. Should my body turn on a short pitch shot?

A. Yes. Even though this shot is played primarily with the hands and arms, the body does turn. Your shoulder turn on the backswing and your weight shift on the follow-through are in proportion to the length of the swing. Your goal is to get the ball up quickly so that it lands on the green from a high trajectory with little roll. In a properly hit pitch shot, a rough rule of thumb is that the ball should carry in the air about two-thirds of the distance and roll only one-third.

Q. Why does a good golfer take a divot with his irons?

A. A good golfer does not try to take a divot—he does it because he starts his downswing in the proper sequence. That is, his lower body initiates the downswing, shifting some of his weight over to the left leg. Then, when the club is released, the clubhead is descending as it strikes the ball and continues to descend slightly after impact. In this way the clubhead reaches the lowest point in the swing after the ball is hit.

Incidentally, when you take divots, check their direction. See if they point toward the target. This is an excellent test of whether or not you are swinging the club in the right direction.

The adviser, the editor, the author, the photographer, the Ping golf bag, and the photographer's assistant.